North American
Historical Atlases

THE WAR
OF 1812

Oliver Hazard Perry records the American victory in the Battle of Lake Erie in the immortal words, "We have met the enemy, and he is ours."

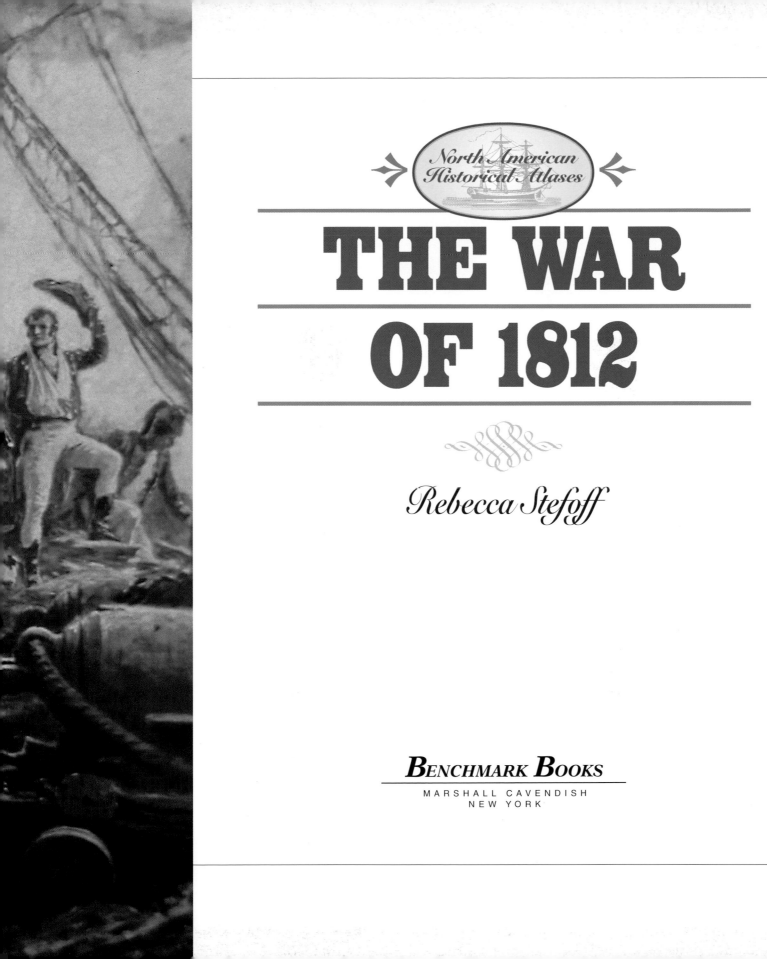

North American Historical Atlases

THE WAR
OF 1812

Rebecca Stefoff

BENCHMARK BOOKS

MARSHALL CAVENDISH
NEW YORK

Benchmark Books
Marshall Cavendish Corporation
99 White Plains Road
Tarrytown, New York 10591

• • •

Library of Congress Cataloging-in-Publication Data
Stefoff, Rebecca, date.
The War of 1812/Rebecca Stefoff
p. cm—(North American Historical Atlases)
Includes bibliographical references (p.) and index.
ISBN 0-7614-1060-0 (lib.bdg.)
1. United States—History—War of 1812—Juvenile literature.
2. United States—History—War of 1812—Maps—Juvenile literature.   I. Title.
E354 .S84   2001   00-020086   973.5'2—dc21

• • •

Printed in Hong Kong
1 3 5 7 8 6 4 2

• • •

Book Designer: Judith Turziano
Photo Researcher: Matthew Dudley

• • •

CREDITS
Front cover: *The Library of Congress Map Division*—map illustrating
the forts and batteries at Plattsburg. September 1814.
Back cover: *Corbis-Bettmann*—Battle of New Orleans.

The photographs and maps in this book are used by permission and through the courtesy of:
Archive Photos: 11, 18, 26–27. *Baldwin H. Ward and Kathryn C. Ward/CORBIS:* 19. *Corbis-Bettmann:* 2–3,
7, 12, 13, 14, 23, 31, 36, 39, 42. *The Library of Congress Maps Division:* 10, 15, 25, 34, 35, 37, 38.

Contents

Chapter One

THE WAY TO WAR

In 1783, Britain and the United States signed the Treaty of Paris, ending the Revolutionary War. But the peace brought by the treaty did not last long. Less than thirty years later, the United States and Great Britain were at war again. Some causes of the War of 1812 were side effects of events in Europe. Other sparks that flared into war were old grievances reaching back to the Revolution. The war included heroic battles on both land and sea—and conflicts over both land and sea lay at the root of it.

Whose Frontier?

The British had never been happy about losing the colonies that became the United States. But they still had Canada, just north of the United States across the St. Lawrence River and the Great Lakes. And they had forts scattered around the Great Lakes. Some of these, like Fort Malden on the shore of Lake Erie, stood on Canadian soil. But other British outposts remained on what was technically U.S. land. After the Revolution, the British had defiantly refused to yield forts at Miami, Niagara, and Detroit in the Northwest Territory. These forts were not only military bases but also centers of trade with the Native Americans of the Ohio River Valley.

Many of those Indians had sided with the British against the Americans during the Revolutionary War. British officers had given them guns, encouraged them to attack American frontier settlements, and even, in a few notorious cases, paid them for the scalps of settlers. The Treaty of Paris ended the open fighting between Great Britain and the United States—at least for a while—but it did not solve the problems of the Indians in the Northwest Territory, whose land was steadily being gobbled up by American settlers. Many of the Americans who pushed into Indian territory paid no attention to treaty borders and completely disregarded Indian claims.

Angry and desperate, some Native Americans turned to their old British **allies** for help. British officers, traders, and agents listened sympathetically to the Indians' complaints about how the Americans were stealing their land, and, in exchange for furs, they gave guns and ammunition to Indian warriors and hunters, knowing that these weapons could be used against American settlers. The British hoped to keep Americans away from the Canadian border and to protect their own interest in the fur trade. If American settlement in the Northwest Territory was kept to a minimum, British traders would continue taking a fortune in beaver and muskrat furs out of the region each year.

In 1794 the United States and Great Britain signed the Jay Treaty, under which the British agreed to give up their forts in American territory. After they did so, Native Americans from the Ohio River Valley and the Great Lakes

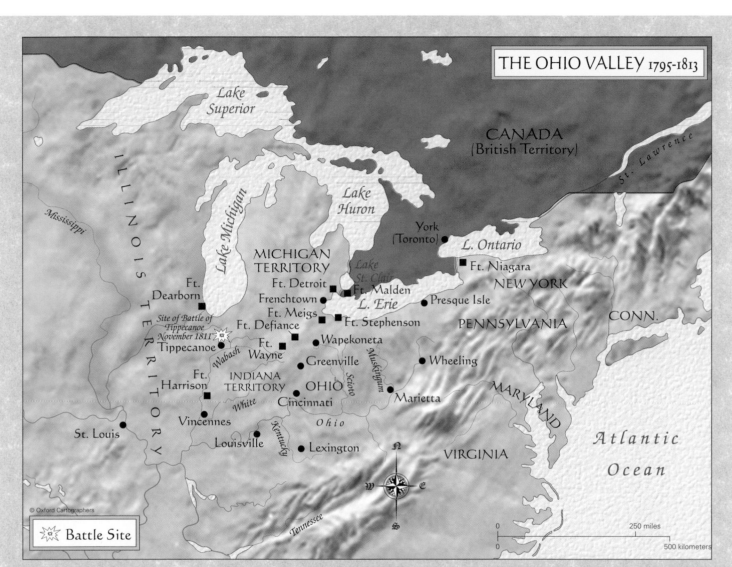

THE OHIO VALLEY 1795-1813

Lake Superior

CANADA (British Territory)

St. Lawrence

Mississippi

Lake Michigan

ILLINOIS TERRITORY

Lake Huron

MICHIGAN TERRITORY

Lake St. Clair

York (Toronto)

L. Ontario

Ft. Niagara

NEW YORK

Ft. Dearborn

Ft. Detroit

Ft. Malden

Frenchtown

L. Erie

Presque Isle

Site of Battle of Tippecanoe November 1811

Ft. Meigs

Ft. Defiance

Ft. Stephenson

PENNSYLVANIA

CONN.

Tippecanoe

Wabash

Ft. Wayne

Wapekoneta

Greenville

Scioto

Muskingum

Wheeling

MARYLAND

Ft. Harrison

INDIANA TERRITORY

OHIO

Cincinnati

White

Marietta

Atlantic Ocean

Vincennes

St. Louis

Kentucky

Ohio

Louisville

Lexington

VIRGINIA

Tennessee

© Oxford Cartographers

Battle Site

0   250 miles
0   500 kilometers

The clash of cultures and the conflicting goals of various nations made the Ohio River Valley a troubled region during the second half of the 1700s and the early 1800s. Before 1763 the French controlled Canada and established forts at Detroit and other sites. When the British gained possession of Canada and the Ohio Valley, the Valley became more turbulent than ever as settlers rushed in from the British colonies on the coast, putting pressure on the Native Americans who lived and hunted in the Valley. After the American Revolution ended in 1783, one of the most urgent problems of the United States was what to do with its new territory, the Ohio River Valley. The British had promised the Native Americans that the Valley would remain theirs, and Native Americans wanted to hold the U.S. government to that promise. But the land hunger of the American settlers drove them into the territory in ever-increasing numbers, and fast-growing towns like Cincinnati, Louisville, and Vincennes sprang up around army posts. The Native Americans' bloody and long-drawn-out struggle to hold onto their land ended in the Battle of Tippecanoe, fought in the Indiana Territory in 1811. As a result of that battle, many Native Americans sided with the British in the War of 1812.

Around 1800 this stretch of the boundary between New York (on the right) and Canada (left) was called the Niagara Frontier. Like other parts of the boundary, it was the scene of frequent clashes between the British (or their Indian allies) and the Americans. After war broke out in 1812, American forces tried several times to invade Canada. In July of 1814, hard-fought battles occurred at Lundy's Lane and Chippewa, shown here in the center of the map. Despite performing well in those encounters, the Americans failed to establish a hold on Canada.

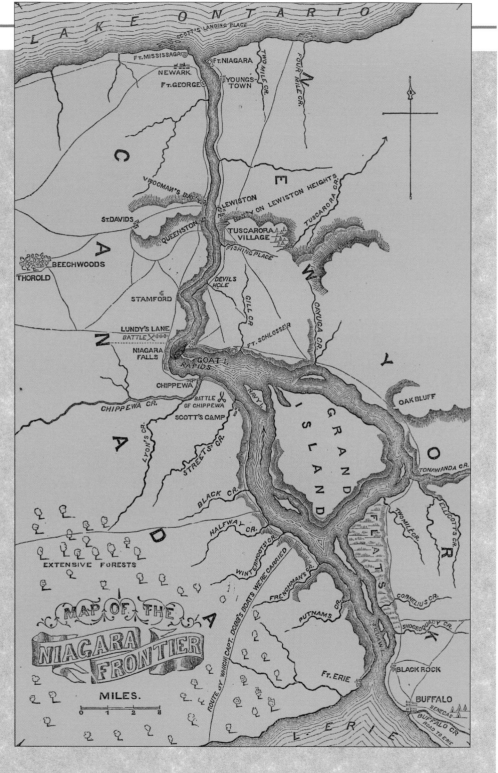

region simply took their trade to Fort Malden. At the fort or traveling through U.S. territory, British agents maintained warm relationships with Indian leaders. Some Indians took this as a sign that the British would help them resist U.S. advances and fight for their land.

TECUMSEH AND THE PROPHET

 Two influential Native Americans in the years leading up to the War of 1812 were a pair of Shawnee brothers from Ohio. Their father and older brother had died fighting white soldiers and settlers, and the two brothers carried on that fight, each in his own way.

Tecumseh was a respected warrior, a skilled **orator**, and a brilliant leader. Beginning around 1789 he led war parties against American settlers. After 1795, believing that **corrupt** Indian leaders had betrayed their people by signing treaties with the U.S. government, Tecumseh made wide-ranging journeys to drum up support among various Native American nations for a **confederacy** that would unite the tribes against the whites.

Lalawethika's path was very different: He was a lazy drunkard until 1805, when he launched a Native American religious movement and became a respected spiritual leader called Tenskwatawa, the Prophet. Claiming to have received messages from

In 1810 the Shawnee leader Tecumseh confronted William Henry Harrison, governor of the Indiana Territory, and warned him that the Native Americans of the Ohio River Valley would give up no more of their land.

the spirit whom the Indians called the Master of Life, Tenskwatawa told his followers to give up all white customs, abandon guns and alcohol, and return to their traditional beliefs and way of life. His powerful spiritual appeal, combined with Tecumseh's shrewd political leadership, made them a force in the Northwest Territory.

Clashes at Sea

While tensions rose on the frontier, the new nation was also having rough sailing on the high seas. Sturdy, swift American ships had begun to play an ever-larger role in world trade, traveling from East Coast harbors to ports in Asia, Africa, Europe, and South America. U.S. **maritime** power increased in the mid-1790s, after Great Britain and France entered into a war that drained their energies. By 1800 the United States had more ships at sea than any

British sailors seize an American and prepare to carry him into unwilling servitude on a British ship. This practice, detested by the American people, was one of the major causes of the War of 1812.

nation except Great Britain, which still considered itself the ruler of the waves.

At first the United States, as a **neutral** nation, traded freely with both Great Britain and France. By 1805, however, both nations had begun interfering with U.S. trade. The British wanted to keep American ships from reaching French ports, and the French had the same idea about **blockading** British ports.

Americans resented these attempts to limit their trade. Even more bitterly they objected to the British practice known as **impressment**, which meant seizing sailors from American vessels to serve in the British navy. Great Britain was short of **naval** manpower, and British captains claimed the right to recapture anyone who had deserted from the British navy. Many of the men seized in this manner, however, were not British deserters but American citizens. More than fifteen thousand were impressed from American ships between 1793 and 1812—three times as many as were in the entire U.S. Navy.

Impressment was a dreadful fate. Discipline in the British navy was extremely harsh. Food was rotten. Chances of death or a crippling injury in battle were high. Sailors' folklore was full of stories about Americans who jumped overboard to drown or who cut off their own hands rather than be impressed.

American citizens grew furious with Great Britain over impressment. Then, in June of 1807, the British warship *Leopard* opened fire

FIGHTING PIRATES IN AFRICA

 The rise of the United States as a naval power did not come without a price. For years European shipping had endured terrorism by pirates who operated out of Tripoli, Tunis, Algiers, and Morocco on the Barbary Coast, as the western coast of North Africa was called. Using the threat of attack, these Barbary states blackmailed ships into paying tribute, a fee that guaranteed safe passage. The United States was now expected to pay up as well. Conflict broke out in 1801 after the ruler of Tripoli increased his demands and President Thomas Jefferson refused to pay. In 1804, the Tripoli pirates captured the U.S. warship *Philadelphia* and imprisoned its crew.

A young American lieutenant named Stephen Decatur sneaked into Tripoli and set fire to the ship rather than let the pirates use her. The following year Tripoli dropped

A dramatic image of Stephen Decatur fending off North African pirates. Although this portrayal is not very realistic, Decatur's deed was genuinely heroic—a British admiral called it "the most bold and daring act of the age."

its demands for tribute. The United States had to pay a large ransom for the release of the captured crewmen, but the power of the Barbary pirates had been broken.

on the American vessel *Chesapeake* because the *Chesapeake's* captain refused to let the *Leopard's* officers search for deserters. Three Americans were killed. The mutterings of outrage against Britain turned to cries demanding war.

Trade Troubles

Jefferson and the U.S. Congress were not quite ready to go to war, but, after the attack on the *Chesapeake*, they took action against Great Britain. In 1807 Congress passed the Embargo Act, a law that forbade Americans to trade—not just with Britain but with *any* other nation. The idea was to prevent British merchants from buying American goods that had passed through a third country.

The Embargo Act was a disaster. It didn't hurt Britain much—the British began buying farm products and timber from South America. But it hit hard at America's shipbuilding and shipping trades. Unemployment and frustration rose, as a poem of the day makes clear:

Our ships all in motion,
Once whitened the ocean;
They sailed and returned with a Cargo.
Now doomed to decay
They are fallen a prey,
To Jefferson, worms, and Embargo.

Feeling against the Embargo Act was so strong in New England, America's maritime center, that some people there wanted to break off from the United States and rejoin Great Britain. Congress **repealed** the Embargo Act in 1809, although other trade laws took its place.

Sparks Fly on the Frontier

The simmering tension on the western frontier now burst into open flame. In 1808 Tecumseh and his brother, the Prophet, founded a settlement called Prophetstown in northern Indiana, on the banks of the Tippecanoe River. It grew steadily larger as unhappy Native Americans from many tribes joined the brothers' following.

William Henry Harrison, governor of the Indiana Territory, feared the growing power of the Indian leaders. He was especially afraid that they would form an alliance with the British in Canada to drive American settlers out of the Ohio River Valley. In 1810 Tecumseh visited the governor to object to a recent treaty

The Battle of Tippecanoe was seen as a great victory for William Henry Harrison, who wiped out a Native American settlement that many frontier settlers regarded as troublesome. In later years Harrison ran successfully for president with the slogan, "Tippecanoe and Tyler [his vice-presidential candidate] too."

that stripped the Indians of still more land and to warn that the Native Americans were uniting to put a halt to future treaties. The following year, learning that Tecumseh was away on a journey, Harrison led an army against Prophetstown and destroyed the settlement.

The Battle of Tippecanoe made Harrison a hero—he would later be elected president on the strength of it—and was seen as an American victory. But it resulted in just what Harrison had feared: It drove Tecumseh and hundreds of his followers straight into the arms of the British in Canada. American settlers in the Northwest Territory, dreading an attack from the north, began demanding a U.S. invasion of Canada. Cries for war were becoming louder.

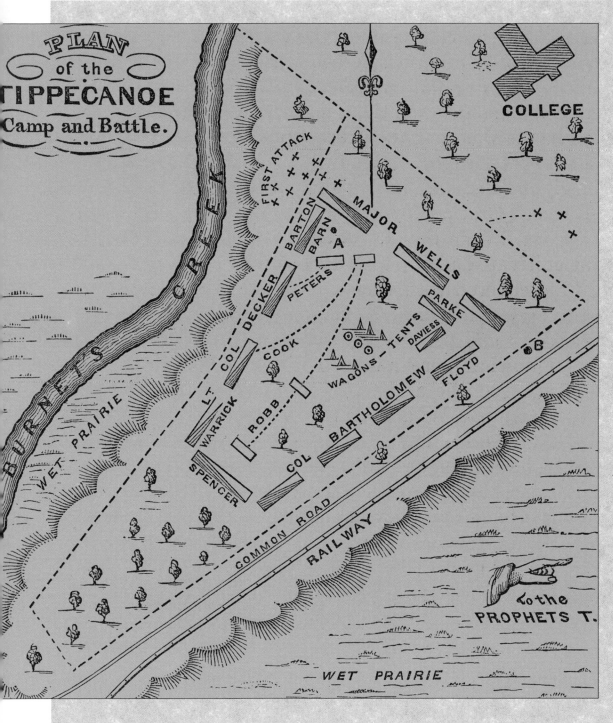

PLAN of the TIPPECANOE Camp and Battle.

BURNETS CREEK

COLLEGE

FIRST ATTACK

WET PRAIRIE

LT. COL DECKER

BARTON

BARN

PETERS

MAJOR

WELLS

A

COOK

WAGONS — TENTS

PARKE

DAVIESS

WARRICK

ROBB

COL

BARTHOLOMEW

FLOYD

B

SPENCER

COMMON ROAD

RAILWAY

to the PROPHETS T.

WET PRAIRIE

Harrison's forces made this camp along a creek that flowed into the Tippecanoe River. (The college, road, and railway did not exist at the time of the battle—instead, the area was wooded and sparsely settled.) Tecumseh's brother, the Prophet, led warriors in what he hoped would be a surprise attack on the camp, but to their dismay the Native Americans found themselves involved in a pitched battle. The Indians retreated, and on the following day Harrison marched to Prophetstown and burned it to the ground.

Chapter Two

A NEW NATION AT WAR

"**F**ree trade and sailors' rights" was the slogan of Americans who wanted to go to war against trade restrictions and impressment. "On to Canada!" shouted those, mostly in the West, who wanted to end British influence on the Indians or even to **annex** Canada's fertile farmlands. Although France had done almost as much as Britain to interfere with U.S. activities abroad, most Americans saw Britain as the greater enemy. After all, just a generation earlier they had been fighting against the British for their very survival, while France had helped them in that struggle. When war came—and even cautious president Madison saw that it *would* come—the United States would test its strength against Great Britain for the second time.

War Hawks in Congress

With the elections of 1810, the United States lurched sharply closer to war. A number of fiery young Republicans from western and southern states won seats in Congress. Their eagerness to challenge Britain had earned them the nickname War Hawks, and they lost no time in strengthening the

James Madison, the fourth president of the United States, presided over the young nation during its first war. Madison had hoped to avoid war, but aggressive members of the U.S. Congress pressured him to test America's strength against Great Britain.

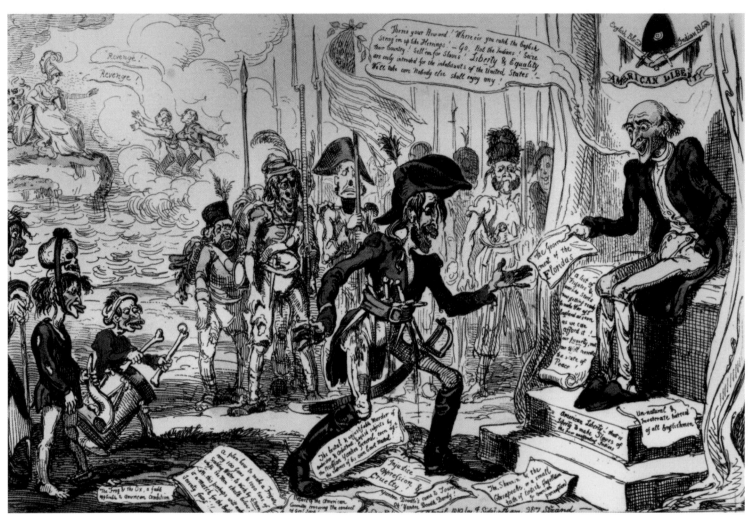

The long-brewing tension between the British and the Americans continued even after the War of 1812 ended. This satirical British political cartoon shows President James Monroe rewarding Andrew Jackson for his war against the Seminole Indians in Florida in 1817-1818. The ghosts crying out for revenge in the background represent two British citizens whom Jackson had executed for helping the Indians—an incident that enraged the British public.

army and the navy, a vital step in preparation for war.

Chief among the War Hawks were Henry Clay of Kentucky, who was elected Speaker of the House of Representatives in 1811; John Calhoun of South Carolina; and Felix Grundy of Tennessee. They spoke for rural Americans —farmers who were suffering economic hardship because they could not sell their crops overseas, and frontier settlers who were convinced that the British were arming the Indians for a bloody assault.

The War Hawks had other motives as well. As Republicans, they believed that victory in war would strengthen their party and make the rival Federalist party, which was strongest in New England and which opposed war, look bad. Another motive was **nationalism**, a form of patriotism or national pride that places strong emphasis on glory, honor, and protecting the interests of one's country at any cost. Benjamin Franklin, the American inventor and publisher who had been a leading **patriot** in Revolutionary times, believed that the United States would one day have to fight for the respect of other nations, especially Britain. Years earlier he had said that "the War of the Revolution has been won, but the War of Independence is still to be fought." The War Hawks, seeing British policies as a humiliating insult to the United States, relentlessly pushed President Madison and Congress to start that fight.

Madison's Declaration

On June 18, 1812, after seven months of debate, Congress declared war on Great Britain. Madison gave as reasons for going to war Britain's impressment of American sailors, its refusal to allow the United States to trade with other European nations, and its support for Indian uprisings on the western frontier.

The War Hawks confidently claimed that the United States would win the war in thirty days. Soon they would discover just how unprepared for war their nation really was. Its seven-thousand-man army consisted mostly of untrained, inexperienced newcomers. Its seven generals were old and out of practice, not having seen combat since the Revolution. Vigorous new officers would emerge during the war, but not immediately. The country also had three-quarters of a million **militiamen**, but they were even less well trained than the soldiers, and they were available only for short periods and only in their home states. The situation was worse with the U.S. Navy, which had only twenty ships compared with Britain's six hundred.

Nor was the United States united in the war effort. People in New England scornfully referred to "Mr. Madison's war" and refused to support it. Some of them even supplied beef cattle to the British in Canada during the war.

Ironically, the war need not have happened —but no one in the United States knew that. Just two days before the U.S. declaration of war, the British Parliament decided to end its practice of impressing sailors from American ships. If Congress had known that one of the principal American grievances had ended, it would most likely have resisted the War Hawks' pressures. But communication across the Atlantic took weeks, and word of Parliament's decision did not arrive until the U.S. had started the war.

MAJOR MILITARY ENGAGEMENTS 1812

Lake Superior

CANADA
(British Territory)

Montréal

St. Lawrence

ILLINOIS TERRITORY

Ft. Mackinac

Lake Huron

Lake Michigan

Kingston

Plattsburg

L. Champlain

York
(Toronto)

L. Ontario

Oswego

Mississippi

MICHIGAN TERRITORY

Lake St. Clair

Queenston

Ft. Niagara

Ft. Detroit

Ft. Malden

NEW YORK

Albany

Ft. Dearborn

Frenchtown

Ft. Meigs

Ft. Stephenson

L. Erie

Buffalo

Erie

CONN.

Hudson

Ft. Defiance

Cleveland

PENNSYLVANIA

Tippecanoe

Tippecanoe

Wapekoneta

Wabash

Ft. Wayne

Greenville

OHIO

Philadelphia

NEW JERSEY

Illinois

Missouri

Ft. Harrison

White

INDIANA TERRITORY

Dayton

Scioto

Muskingum

Potomac

Baltimore

MARYLAND

DELAWARE

Cincinnati

Kentucky

Ohio

Washington

Atlantic Ocean

N

VIRGINIA

Tennessee

© Oxford Cartographers

Battle Site
American Movements
British Movements

W E
S

0   250 miles
0   500 kilometers

The United States declared war on Great Britain but expected to do most of the fighting in Canada. Their major plan was to invade their northern neighbor. In 1812, U.S. forces tried to enter Canada from Detroit, Niagara, and Lake Champlain. Each attempt ended in complete disaster. The conflict was only in its second month when General William Hull surrendered Fort Detroit and its 2,000 men to the British—not an encouraging beginning for the Americans who had pushed the country into war.

The tide of war turned in 1813, when the Americans won two important victories. One was the Battle of Lake Erie, which ended British control of the lake and dramatically changed the course of the Canadian campaign. Upon hearing of the British defeat on the lake, the British commander at Fort Malden, Brigadier General Henry Procter, knew that the Americans would immediately cross the lake. Procter led his 600 soldiers in a frantic retreat up the Thames River, chased by William Henry Harrison and 3,500 American troops. Along with Procter traveled about a thousand Indians who had allied themselves with the British. When the Americans caught up with them, Procter escaped, but many of his men were captured. Tecumseh, the leader of the Native Americans, fell in battle. Americans call this clash the Battle of the Thames, but to Canadians it is known as the Battle of Moraviantown. The name comes from a nearby settlement of Christian Indians. After overcoming Procter's force, the Americans destroyed Moraviantown.

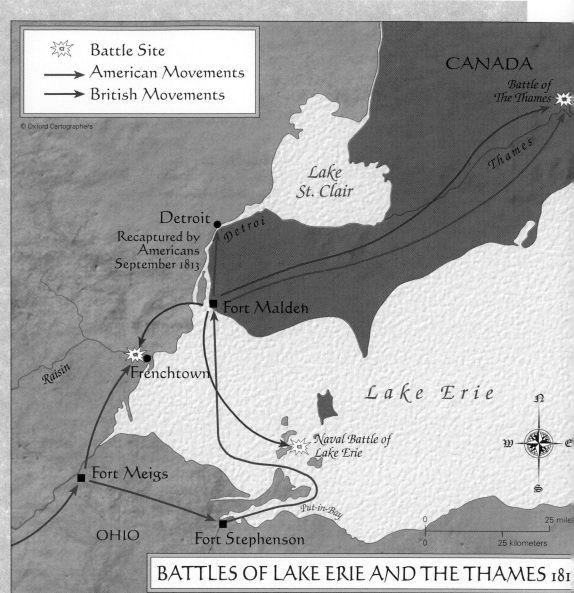

BATTLES OF LAKE ERIE AND THE THAMES 181

A British officer yields his sword in surrender after Oliver Hazard Perry's destruction of Britain's Lake Erie fleet. The Battle of Lake Erie boosted American confidence and shook that of the British.

The Canadian Campaign

Knowing that most of Britain's military might was locked up in its titanic war with France, the American commanders decided on a bold offense in the hope of winning a quick victory. They decided to attack Canada.

General William Hull led the American force from Detroit toward Fort Malden. His advance was too cautious and slow, however. A British general named Isaac Brock, with whom Tecumseh's warriors were allied, forced Hull to retreat to Detroit and then surrounded the fort there. Hull surrendered. Several other American forts on the Great Lakes also fell. Two other attempted American attacks on Canada failed because militiamen refused to fight out-

THE DEATH OF TECUMSEH

 The Battle of the Thames was a crushing defeat for the Indians who had joined forces with the British Canadians. When General Harrison's troops attacked the retreating British and Indian column, the British fled headlong. The Indians stood and tried to fight, but they were overwhelmed. Tecumseh was one of many who fell on the field of battle. His death ended the dream of a Native American confederacy, and it discouraged his surviving followers, most of whom gave up the fight. They rightly predicted that the Americans would win the War of 1812, and they hoped only that the United States would not punish them too harshly for having fought on the side of the British.

On this early map of the Battle of the Thames, the legend "Tecumtha Fell" marks the spot where the Shawnee leader Tecumseh was said to have died in battle. His body, however, was never identified, and, in the years after the war, some Native Americans clung to the myth that he had escaped death on the battlefield and would one day return to lead them again. In reality, however, he was most likely buried in a secret location by loyal followers.

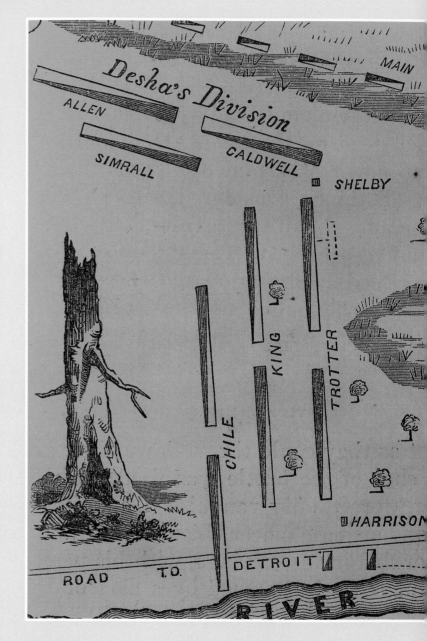

Large Swamp

INDIANS

THOMPSON

SPIES

JOHNSON

BRITISH AND INDIANS

TECUMTHA FELL

Small Swamp

R.M.JOHNSON

J.JOHNSON

SPIES

BRITISH

PROCTOR

CANNON

PAUL AND INDIANS

THAMES

side the United States. The war's opening stroke, the bold plan to invade the enemy's territory, was an utter failure, and several generals were revealed as incompetent or cowardly.

Too late, the Americans realized that Canada was untouchable as long as the British could swiftly move their troops by water. The second phase of the Canadian campaign, in 1813, focused on gaining control of Lake Erie. A young naval officer named Oliver Hazard Perry was assigned to oversee the building of a fleet and to capture Lake Erie. He quelled a shipbuilders' strike, got a half dozen vessels in the water, and confronted the nine-ship British lake fleet on September 10. Fighting under a banner bearing the words "Don't Give Up the Ship," Perry's tough little squadron survived the near-destruction of one flagship to win the day. "We have met the enemy, and he is ours," Perry wrote to General William Henry Harrison after his victory in the U.S. Navy's first sea battle.

The same year brought other successes on Canadian soil. In April, American forces attacked York (now Toronto) and burned some government buildings, although they could not hold the city. In October, they were victorious over a combined Canadian and Native American force in the Battle of the Thames. U.S. troops failed dismally, however, to capture the fortified city of Montreal, and they could not prevent British forces from attacking Fort Niagara and Buffalo in New York.

The War at Sea

The U.S. Navy was small, but three of its warships were among the fastest on the seven seas. One of them was the *Constitution*, which outfought two British warships in 1812. In August she captured the British **frigate** *Guerriere* in the North Atlantic Ocean. Later she destroyed Britain's *Java* in the waters off Brazil. After seeing an enemy shot bounce off the *Constitution's* hull during one of these battles, an American sailor nicknamed the ship "Old Ironsides," and the name stuck.

Two smaller vessels, the *Wasp* and the *Hornet*, harassed British naval ships. A popular cartoon in the United States showed a fat man representing John Bull, a symbol for Great Britain, being painfully stung by a wasp and a hornet. In October, the *United States*, under the command of Stephen Decatur, defeated and captured the British warship *Macedonian*, bringing her back to Connecticut, where she was made into a U.S. Navy ship.

A battle between the British frigate *Shannon* and the U.S. frigate *Chesapeake*—the same ship that the *Leopard* had attacked—did not end so well for the Americans. In June of 1813, outside Boston Harbor, the *Shannon* captured the *Chesapeake*. The American captain, James Lawrence, was fatally wounded in the fighting. His last words to his men were "Don't give up the ship!"—words his friend Perry would use to inspire the Lake Erie fleet a few months later.

The American vessel **Constitution** *(left) defeating and capturing the British* **Guerriere**. *The* **Constitution**, *preserved today as a national monument, was one of the more successful American ships during the war.*

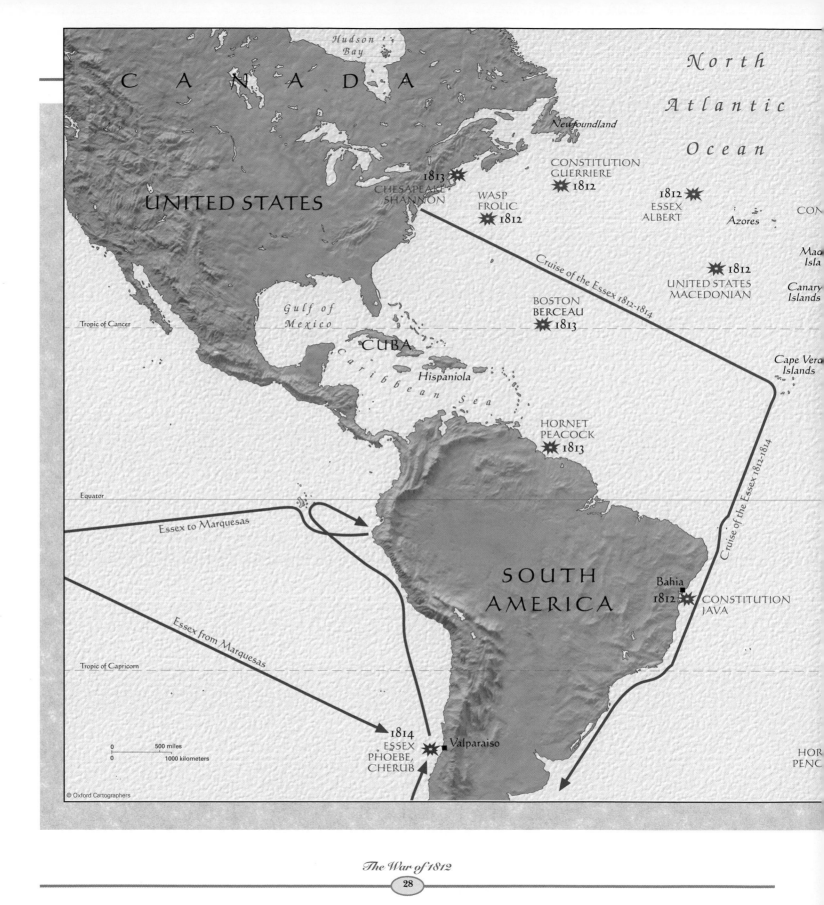

Hudson
Bay

C A N A D A

Newfoundland

North

Atlantic

Ocean

UNITED STATES

1813 ✳
CHESAPEAKE
SHANNON

WASP
FROLIC
✳ 1812

CONSTITUTION
GUERRIERE
✳ 1812

1812 ✳
ESSEX
ALBERT

Azores

CON

Mad
Isla

1812 ✳
UNITED STATES
MACEDONIAN

Canary
Islands

Tropic of Cancer

Gulf of
Mexico

BOSTON
BERCEAU
✳ 1813

Cape Verd
Islands

CUBA

Hispaniola

Caribbean Sea

HORNET
PEACOCK
✳ 1813

Cruise of the Essex 1812-1814

Equator

Essex to Marquesas

SOUTH
AMERICA

Bahia ■
1812 ✳
CONSTITUTION
JAVA

Cruise of the Essex 1812-1814

Essex from Marquesas

Tropic of Capricorn

0   500 miles
0   1000 kilometers

1814
ESSEX
PHOEBE,
CHERUB ✳ ■ Valparaiso

HOR
PENC

© Oxford Cartographers

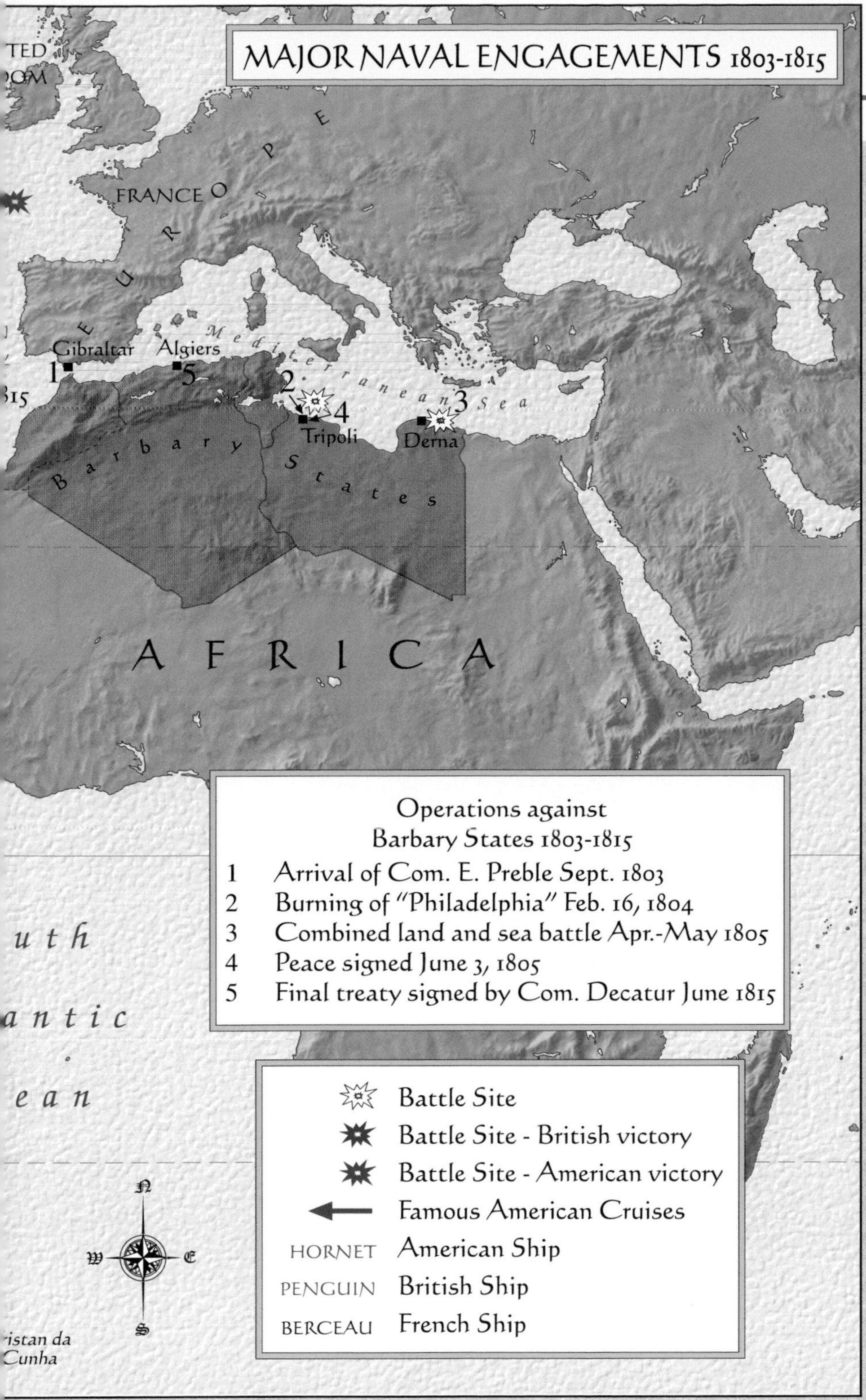

FRANCE

EUROPE

Mediterranean Sea

Gibraltar   Algiers
1   5   2
                    4   3
                Tripoli   Derna

Barbary   States

AFRICA

uth

antic

ean

ristan da
Cunha

Operations against Barbary States 1803-1815

1   Arrival of Com. E. Preble Sept. 1803
2   Burning of "Philadelphia" Feb. 16, 1804
3   Combined land and sea battle Apr.-May 1805
4   Peace signed June 3, 1805
5   Final treaty signed by Com. Decatur June 1815

✴   Battle Site
✴   Battle Site - British victory
✴   Battle Site - American victory
←   Famous American Cruises
HORNET   American Ship
PENGUIN   British Ship
BERCEAU   French Ship

The history of the U.S. war against the Barbary pirates is shown on the right-hand portion of the this map, while the central and left-hand portions show the important naval engagements between the Americans (in blue) and the British (in red) during the War of 1812. The blue line indicates the long voyage of the Essex, an American ship that cruised through most of the Atlantic and Pacific during the war and finally fought two British ships off the coast of South America in 1814. During the course of the war, American vessels won many of their duels with enemy ships and caused heavy damage to British trade. These victories raised American spirits but did not pose a serious threat to British control of the seas.

Chapter Three

WAR'S END

In late 1812 the British responded to U.S. victories at sea with a massive blockade of the American East Coast. They left New England free, hoping that the New Englanders would join them. By 1814, however, they realized that New England would remain part of the United States, even if its support for the American war effort was feeble, so they extended their blockade to blanket the entire coast. In the third year of the war, only a few American ships traveled the seas—the rest were bottled up in port. That same year, Great Britain ended its long war with France. Now the British could concentrate fully on their conflict with the Americans. The War of 1812 entered a new phase.

The British Take Action

Great Britain added fourteen thousand troops to its army in North America and planned a three-pronged attack on the United States. One attack would move south from Canada across Lake Champlain into northern New York State. Another would advance up the Chesapeake Bay to attack Washington and Baltimore. The third would strike at New Orleans to gain control of the Mississippi River mouth.

On paper the British plan looked good. But the American fighting force had improved and grown larger in two years of fighting. Even before the British set their plan in motion, an American force invaded Canada and defeated British troops at the Battle of Chippewa. The

Americans soon withdrew, but when the British came at them across Lake Champlain, a small American naval force succeeded in destroying all but one of the British vessels. At the same time, American soldiers turned back a much larger invasion force at Plattsburg, New York. The British attack from the north was a failure.

The Battle Against the Creek Nation

Tecumseh's death did not end Native American participation in the war. He had worked to enlist the Creek nation of Alabama and Mississippi in his confederacy, and the Creeks had sided with the British. In August of 1813 they had attacked U.S. Fort Mims in Mississippi, killing hundreds of people. Both the federal government and the western settlers wanted the Creek uprising crushed.

Andrew Jackson, a Tennessee militia leader, took on that challenge. He led two thousand men into Creek country and destroyed a major force of Creeks and their Cherokee allies in the Battle of Horseshoe Bend in March of 1814. This defeat forced the surviving Creeks to give up most of their traditional homeland. And it made a popular hero out of Jackson, who, like Harrison, would one day become president.

Washington Ablaze

In August of 1814 the British launched their attack on the Chesapeake Bay. Frigates sailed up the Potomac and Patuxent rivers, as did

MAJOR MILITARY ENGAGEMENTS 1813

Lake Superior

Montréal

CANADA
(British Territory)

Plattsburg

Kingston

Ft. Mackinac

Lake Huron

York (Toronto)

St. Lawrence

Sacketts Harbor

L. Ontario

Oswego

MICHIGAN TERRITORY

Fort Niagara

NEW YORK

Albany

Queenston

Ft. Detroit

L. Erie

Buffalo

CONN.

Frenchtown

Erie

Ft. Meigs

Cleveland

Ft. Dearborn

Illinois

Ft. Defiance

Ft. Stephenson

PENNSYLVANIA

Ft. Wayne

Wapekoneta

ILLINOIS TERRITORY

Tippecanoe

INDIANA TERRITORY

Greenville

OHIO

Philadelphia

MARYLAND

NEW JERSEY

Baltimore

Ft. Harrison

Dayton

Potomac

DELAWARE

White

Cincinnati

Dayton

Washington

MISSOURI TERRITORY

Missouri

Ohio

Kentucky

VIRGINIA

James

KENTUCKY

Cumberland

Tennessee

NORTH CAROLINA

TENNESSEE

Huntsville

Ft. Deposit

Creek War 1813-1814

SOUTH CAROLINA

Savannah

Charleston

Atlantic Ocean

MISSISSIPPI TERRITORY

Mississippi

Alabama

Vicksburg

GEORGIA

Savannah

BRITISH BLOCKADE

LOUISIANA

Mobile

Ft. Mims

New Orleans

Pensacola

FLORIDA (Spain)

Gulf of Mexico

0   250 miles
0   500 kilometers

Battle Site
American Movements
British Movements
British Blockade

ord Cartographers

Although 1813 brought some significant American victories along the Canadian border, it also brought a blockade—a line of British ships that patrolled the Atlantic coast, keeping both military and trade vessels from entering and leaving American ports. The blockade not only bottled up ships that might have attacked British shipping, it also brought economic hardship to farmers who could not ship their products to markets and to merchants who could not obtain imported goods. At first the British left New England free of the blockade, hoping that the New Englanders would split off from the rest of the country and join the war on the British side. Although President Madison worried that some people in New England wanted to do so, the region remained loyal, and in 1814 Great Britain enlarged the blockade to include New England.

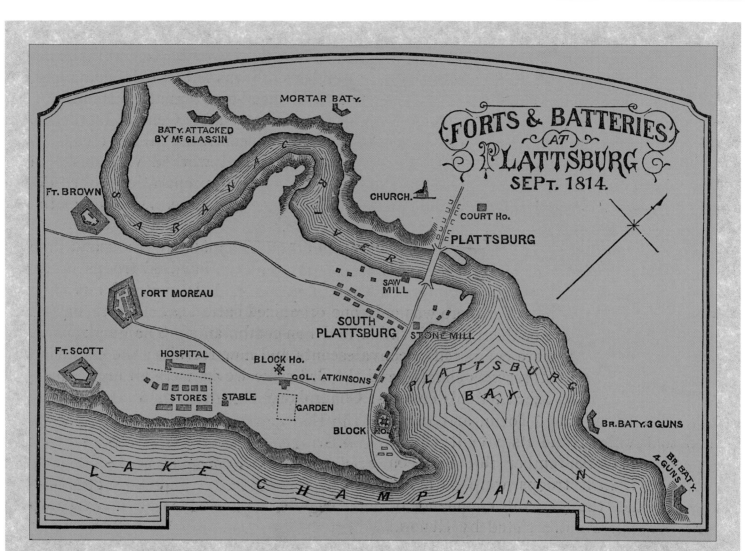

In September of 1814, the British launched an invasion of New York. More than
10,000 troops, commanded by General Sir George Prevost, moved south from Canada
to Plattsburg on Lake Champlain. Despite the advantages of a larger force,
mounted troops, more and better guns, and highly trained officers and soldiers,
the British not only failed to capture the town but were defeated by the
determined Americans. Prevost retreated back to Canada. News of his defeat
at Plattsburg convinced the British government to end the costly War of 1812.

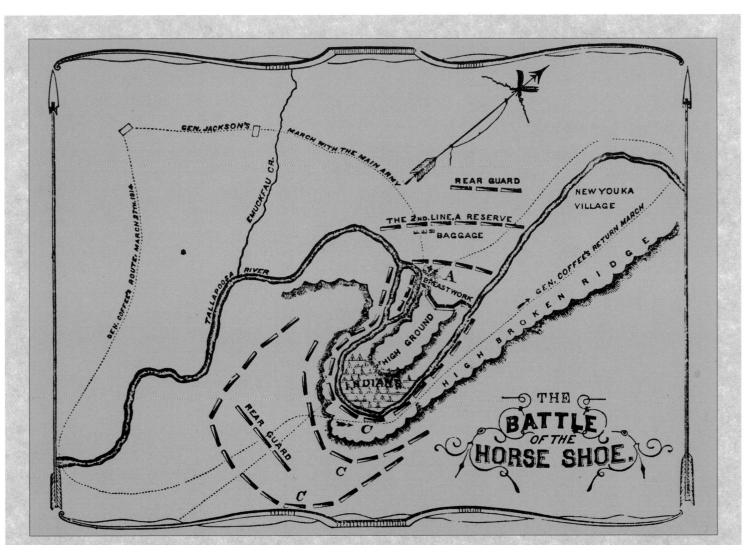

A map from an 1868 history of the War of 1812 shows the setting of the Battle of Horseshoe Bend, where Andrew Jackson won a crushing victory over the Creek Indians. The letter A indicates a hilltop from which Jackson's cannon fired down upon the Native American village, shown by the rows of tepees in the bend of the river. The Indians had built their village here thinking that the river offered protection, but when Jackson attacked with cannon they found themselves trapped, with no escape route.

barges carrying 4,000 red-coated British troopers. They landed and advanced on the nation's capital, Washington, D.C. A mixed force of militia, soldiers, and sailors tried to stop them at Bladensburg and other points along their march, but the British stormed onward. As they approached the capital, President Madison and other government officials fled the city.

Remembering the damage done by the Americans in York, the British set fire to gov-

Having attacked a number of sites on the shores of the Chesapeake Bay, the British invaded Washington, D.C., and spent a day trying to destroy the American capital. The capture of Washington may have seemed like a major victory for the British, but they failed to hold onto the city, and the following month British forces suffered serious setbacks at Baltimore and Plattsburg.

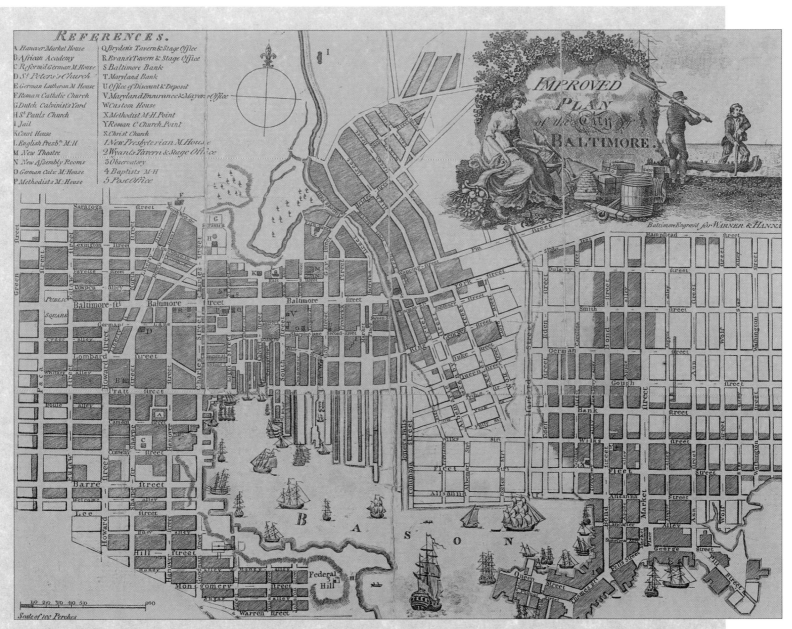

An 1804 city plan of Baltimore shows the busy harbor at the heart of the city, with vessels lined up at its docks. Although smaller and less prosperous than Boston, New York, or Philadelphia, Baltimore was a significant center of shipping whose destruction would have been a blow to American commerce.

THE WHITE HOUSE

 One of the buildings torched by the British in their attack on Washington was the President's House, or President's Palace, as it was sometimes called. It was also sometimes called the White House, because it was made of pale limestone, unlike most other buildings in Washington, which were of built of red brick. The President's House was a stately structure on Pennsylvania Avenue, although it was surrounded by muddy roads and a swamp. The Madisons had just completed furnishing it when the war broke out. Dolley Madison, the president's wife, kept cool as the redcoats approached. She refused to leave her home until the last possible moment, and she took with her a number of national treasures, including a portrait of George Washington and a copy of the

A British map of Washington, D.C. The caption reads, in part, "[A] fine city of the United States of America…. It was taken by the British Forces…on the 24th Aug. 1814, who, having burnt the Presidents Palace, the Capitol & all the Public Buildings etc. abandoned it."

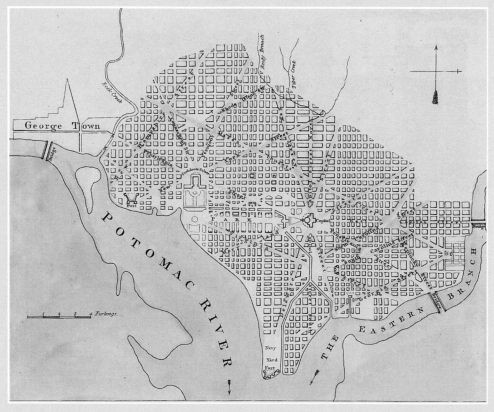

After leaving Washington, the British sailed to Baltimore. On September 13-14, shells flew between the American troops in Fort McHenry and the British fleet trying to enter Baltimore Harbor. The American defenders succeeded in keeping the British from landing, and Baltimore was spared the dire fate that had fallen on the nation's capital.

Declaration of Independence. Later she supervised the repair of the building after the British burning. She had it painted white to cover the scorch marks left on its walls, and from that time the name "White House" came into wider use. In 1901 President Theodore Roosevelt made it the official name of the president's residence.

ernment buildings. In the Capitol building they used axes to hack desks and chairs in the chambers of the Senate and House of Representatives, then used gunpowder and rockets to set the place on fire. To the regret of the British, a thunderstorm put out most of the fires before they had completely destroyed the structures. The next day the British withdrew, leaving a gutted capital behind them.

The British might have hurt the American cause if they had held Washington. Instead they abandoned the city and focused their next attack on Baltimore, to the north. But Baltimore was better prepared than Washington and managed to fight off the attack, which occurred in the middle of September, just about the time the Americans were trouncing the British at Plattsburg. Shells fired from Fort McHenry prevented the British from approaching the town. The defense of Fort McHenry also inspired a young American lawyer named Francis Scott Key to write "The Star-Spangled Banner," which became the American national anthem.

Showdown in New Orleans

Only one part of the British plan remained: the attack on New Orleans. But by August of 1814 representatives of the British and American governments were meeting in Ghent, a city in Belgium, seeking a way to end the war at the conference table rather than on the battlefield.

At first the British made some strong

The land battles of the first part of the War of 1812 were concentrated in the Great Lakes region. The second part of the conflict, however, saw major battles in the far north (Plattsburg), along the Atlantic coast (the Chesapeake invasion), and in the south. The American military, which had been inexperienced, under-equipped, and unprepared when the United States started the war, became considerably more efficient, effective, and professional as the fighting continued. By the time of the Battle of New Orleans, Americans had successfully defended their new nation against its former owner.

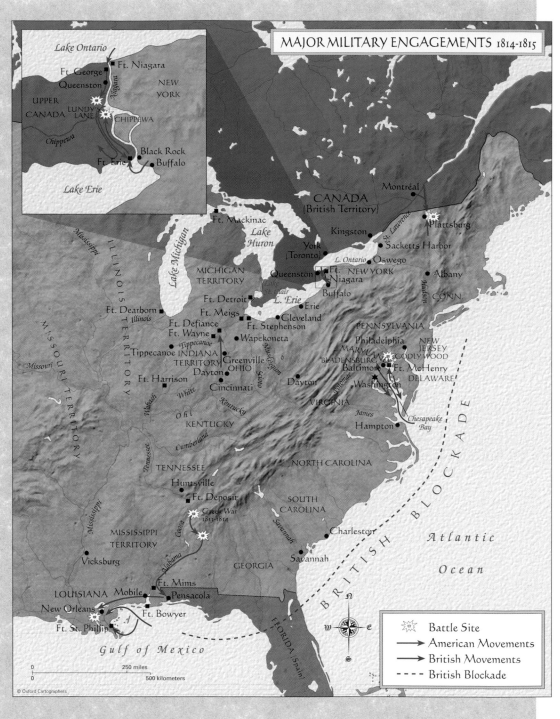

MAJOR MILITARY ENGAGEMENTS 1814-1815

Battle Site
American Movements
British Movements
British Blockade

© Oxford Cartographers

demands: a large reservation for their Indian allies in the Northwest Territory, British forts on U.S. soil, and the annexation by Canada of some territory in northern New England. Word of the American victories at Plattsburg and Baltimore led the British to drop these demands. Now they just wanted to end the war, which they had decided was too costly and troublesome to pursue. So, on December 24, 1814, the two sides signed the Treaty of Ghent. The same communcations delay that had allowed the war to start, however, now kept it going. Word of the treaty did not reach the United States in time to prevent the final battle of the War of 1812—and the biggest American triumph.

On January 8, 1815, a British army of more than 5,000 men marched on New Orleans. The city was defended by Andrew Jackson and more than 4,000 troops, including a number of highly skilled riflemen from Kentucky, where good marksmanship was considered one of the highest virtues. In just an hour the American force killed or wounded more than 2,000 of the redcoats, forcing the survivors to retreat. It was a humiliating defeat for the British, and the War Hawks led the cheering.

Winners and Losers

Congress approved the Treaty of Ghent on February 16, 1815. The American people were overjoyed by the official end of the war. But had they won?

PATRIOTIC PIRATES

Jackson found an unexpected ally in his defense of New Orleans. Jean and Pierre Lafitte, leaders of a pirate band that lurked in the Louisiana waterways and preyed on Spanish ships leaving Mexico, offered their services. Jackson at first turned them down, declaring that he had no use for bandits. But Jean Lafitte persuaded him that the pirates could be useful, and indeed they fought boldly along the barricade that Jackson had built across the road to New Orleans.

Some historians call the War of 1812 "the war nobody won." The Treaty of Ghent simply restored things to exactly the way they had been before the war. Neither Great Britain nor the United States had gained or lost a thing— except the thousands of people killed or wounded in the fighting and the money spent on the war. Even the burning issue of impressment was ignored in the treaty, although the British had already dropped the practice and it never again became a serious problem.

The biggest losers of the War of 1812 were the Native Americans, who had lost some

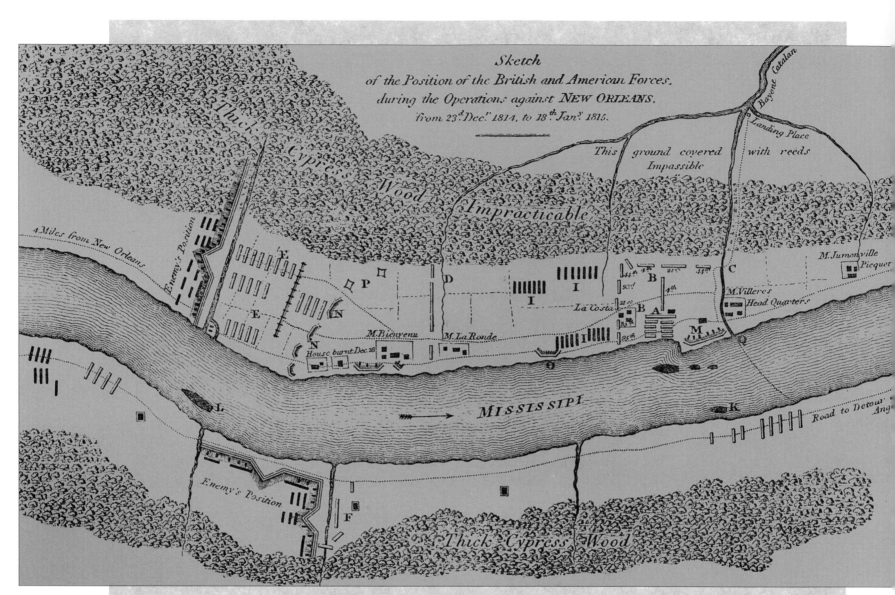

Although the close-in fighting between British and American troops in the Battle of
New Orleans lasted less than a day, preparations for the battle stretched over several weeks.
This map shows the British (labeled "Enemy's Position") lined up outside American fortifications
(on the left-hand side of the plan). The dotted lines represent roads, and the bars across them
are the barricades that Andrew Jackson ordered made to hinder the movement of British troops.

important leaders and a considerable amount of land east of the Mississippi River. Although Indian unrest would still flare up in that part of the country from time to time, the spirit of large-scale resistance had been broken. After the War of 1812, the British in Canada withdrew their support from the Indians of the United States.

Perhaps the only thing that the United States really won in the War of 1812 was international respect and prestige. No longer seen as merely a breakaway British colony or an upstart republic, the United States began to emerge as a world power. Its performance in the war contributed to that power. As a British naval lieutenant remarked in 1829, no one would ever want to fight the Americans except for the honor to be gained "by overcoming an enemy so brave, determined, and alert, and in every way worthy of one's steel, as they have always proved."

Glossary

allies: Parties that have agreed to fight on the same side against an enemy they have in common.

annex: To enlarge a nation or state by adding territory that was formerly outside its borders.

blockading: To block vessels from entering or leaving a port, usually by setting up a protective ring of ships; also to close off a city, town, or district, preventing all imports and exports.

confederacy: Union of states or nations that share some aspects of government or foreign relations but remain individually independent.

corrupt: Lacking in virtue or morality, usually applied to those who give up principles for money or power.

frigate: Warship.

impressment: Forcing people into service.

maritime: Having to do with the sea and shipping.

militiamen: Members of militia, volunteer civilian forces that can be called into military service in times of emergency.

nationalism: Putting the interests of one's own nation above all other concerns.

naval: Having to do with a navy.

neutral: Not taking sides.

orator: Public speaker.

patriot: One who favored American independence from Great Britain.

repealed: Cancelled or overturned.

Map List

ABOUT THE HISTORICAL MAPS

The historical maps used in this book are primary source documents found in The Library of Congress Map Division. You will find these maps on pages 10, 15, 24–25, 34, 35, 37 and 38.

Chronology

1783 Treaty of Paris sets U.S. and British borders in North America.

1801-1805 United States is in conflict with the Barbary Coast states of North Africa. Great Britain and France, at war with one another, try to limit American shipping and trade.

1807 British ship *Leopard* attacks American ship *Chesapeake* in a conflict over British demands to search U.S. vessels.

1807 U.S. Congress passes the Embargo Act to end trade with Great Britain.

1808 Shawnee leaders Tecumseh and Tenskwatawa found Prophetstown.

1809 Repeal of the Embargo Act.

1810 War Hawks are elected to U.S. Congress; Tecumseh confronts territorial governor William Henry Harrison with objections to treaties.

1811 Harrison defeats Native American forces in the Battle of Tippecanoe.

1812 United States declares war on Great Britain; U.S. attempts to invade Canada; Tecumseh allies Native American forces with the British in Canada; *Constitution* is victorious in two naval battles.

1813 Oliver Hazard Perry and U.S. naval forces defeat the British on Lake Erie; Tecumseh is killed in Battle of the Thames; Americans attack Toronto.

1814 Andrew Jackson defeats the Creek Native American nation in the Battle of Horseshoe Bend; British forces burn Washington, D.C., and launch attacks around Chesapeake Bay and in northern New York State; Great Britain and United States make peace with the Treaty of Ghent.

1815 Americans win belated the Battle of New Orleans.

Further Reading

Marrin, Albert. *1812: The War Nobody Won.* New York: Atheneum, 1985.

Morris, Richard B. *The War of 1812.* Minneapolis: Lerner Publications, 1985.

Shorto, Russell T. *Tecumseh and the Dream of an American Indian Nation.* Englewood Cliffs, NJ: Silver Burdett, 1989.

Stefoff, Rebecca. *Tecumseh and the Shawnee Confederation.* New York: Facts On File, 1998.

Stein, R. Conrad. *The Story of the Barbary Pirates.* Chicago: Children's Press, 1982.

Stein, R. Conrad. *The Story of the Burning of Washington.* Chicago: Children's Press, 1984.

WEBSITES

www.militaryheritage.com/1812.htm
(articles, books, reviews, images, and links)

www.cfcsc.dnd.ca/links/milhistory.1812.htm
(maintained by the Information Resource Center of the Canadian Forces College)

ABOUT THE AUTHOR

Rebecca Stefoff is the Oregon-based author of a number of nonfiction books for children and young adults. She has written about many topics in American history, including exploration, the colonies, the Revolutionary War, and the settling of the West. In addition to other volumes in the North American Historical Atlases series, her publications on these subjects include *Women Pioneers* (1995), *Children of the Westward Trail* (1996), and *The Oregon Trail* (1997), as well as several biographies of presidents. In *William Henry Harrison* (1990) and *Tecumseh and the Shawnee Confederation* (1998) she wrote about British-American-Indian relations in the Northwest Territory and about Tecumseh's role in the War of 1812.

Index

Entries are filed letter-by-letter. Page numbers for illustrations and maps are in boldface.